Original title:
Tidepool Wonders

Copyright © 2025 Creative Arts Management OÜ
All rights reserved.

Author: Franklin Stone
ISBN HARDBACK: 978-1-80587-290-0
ISBN PAPERBACK: 978-1-80587-760-8

Shoreline Serenade of the Brave

A crab with shades struts with flair,
Not a care in the world, oh how he dares!
He clicks his claws to the beat of the waves,
While seagulls gossip about beachy knaves.

Starfish play cards, with laughs so loud,
Risky bets made, they've drawn quite a crowd.
Who knew the sand could play host to such fun?
In this wild little world, we've all quite begun!

Whispers of the Shore

A starfish whispers to the shy little snail,
"Did you hear the tales of the giant sea whale?"
The snail looks puzzled, then shrinks in surprise,
As jellyfish dance 'neath the sunlit skies.

Crabs tell jokes that can crack a shell,
"Why do clowns love the ocean so well?"
"Oh crabby! Because it's a real swell tide,
And the seaweed's great for a comedic slide!"

Secrets Beneath the Surf

At dawn, the otters engage in a race,
But they trip over rocks, oh, what a disgrace!
The secrets they share, as they tumble and roll,
Leave their friends laughing, it's a comical goal.

An octopus observes with eight eyes so wise,
With a wink and a swirl, they start to improvise.
"Who needs a stage when you've got the sea?
Just bring your best moves, and come dance with me!"

Dance of the Anemones

Anemones sway in a colorful throng,
With the sea breeze playing their favorite song.
"Let's do the cha-cha!" calls out a bright yellow,
As they twirl and giggle, each one a good fellow.

A fish swims by, quite puzzled and baffled,
"Is this a party, or am I just frazzled?"
But soon he's caught up in the vibrant delight,
Joining the dance, oh what a silly sight!

Secrets of the Shallow Shore

Beneath the seaweed, critters play,
A fish with glasses, hipster in a way.
Starfish doing yoga, striking a pose,
While snails race fast, wearing tiny clothes.

The crabs are gossiping, who wore it best?
A hermit crab's shell beats the rest.
Everyone's twerking, or so they claim,
But all I can see is the opening game!

Symphony of Sea Anemones

Anemones dance, trying to catch a breeze,
With tentacles swaying, like jellyfish tease.
They hum little tunes, quite out of tune,
While clownfish giggle, 'time for a cartoon!'

Mussels form bands, playing shells with flair,
Cranky old oysters just don't seem to care.
But the sea urchins, a prickly choir,
Scream out loud, 'We're more than just spire!'

Where Barnacles Whisper

Barnacles chatter, gossiping so sweet,
'Have you heard the news? They're off their feet!'
The sea is a stage, with creatures so bold,
With tales of adventure that never get old.

A silly old seagull, dressed up in socks,
Calls to the shells, 'Hey, watch for the rocks!'
And all of the mussels, clapping along,
Join in the fun, composing a song!

Crabs in the Painted Grotto

In the grotto where colors collide,
Crabs wear top hats, grinning with pride.
'Let's do a dance!' one shouts with flair,
While others juggle seaweed without a care.

They topple and tumble, it's quite a sight,
With clams playing drums, echoing delight.
As fishes laugh and dolphins hover,
'Who knew crabs could be such a cover!'

Life in a Saltwater Glass

Crabs wear hats made of seaweed,
As fish parade in their own stampede.
Starfish with shades, oh what a sight,
Aquatic party from morning to night.

Shrimp do the cha-cha, clams hold the beat,
Anemones sway, can't find their feet.
Pufferfish puff with an elegant flair,
While sea cucumbers just sit and stare.

Dwellers Among the Rocks

Seashells gossip, oh what a chat,
About the day's tide, and this and that.
Limpets cling tight, don't want to fall,
With barnacles laughing, they're having a ball.

A sea urchin grins, wearing a crown,
While lobsters trade jokes, trying not to frown.
A seaweed band plays tunes so grand,
While a sneaky octopus makes off with a hand.

The Dance of the Dunes

Sand dollars waltz on the breeze so light,
As crabs throw a bash under the moonlight.
Seagulls squawk secrets, flutter and dive,
While starfish dream of their own jive.

The tide pulls back, and the fish make a dash,
Shells snap selfies, oh what a flash!
Barnacles boogie, all snug on the rocks,
While a lonely sea turtle plays hopscotch.

Enigmas of the Marine Depths

Underwater creatures with tales of old,
Unraveling mysteries, both funny and bold.
A grouper gossips about a fishy fate,
While clownfish chuckle, they just can't wait.

The deep sea giggles with jellyfish sway,
As seahorses trot in their own ballet.
Crank up the giggles, let laughter unfold,
In this watery world, everybody's gold.

Crabs in the Moonlight

Under the moon, crabs dance around,
Pinching each other without making a sound.
One found a shell, thought it a crown,
Wobbling proudly, then fell right down.

Lobsters watched closely, giggling a lot,
As one crab tried to show off his spot.
He stumbled and fumbled, tripping on sand,
"Next time," he muttered, "I'll stick to my stand!"

Symphony of the Sea Stars

Sea stars gather for their big debut,
With arms that wiggle and twinkle, it's true.
They call it a symphony, oh what a sight,
But off-key they sing, much to our delight.

One forgot the tune, and started to jig,
The others all laughed; he was quite the big rig.
With five floppy limbs, he spun in a swirl,
While seaweed and sand joined the nautical twirl.

Fragile Lives on the Edge

At the water's edge, where wet meets the dry,
Little critters wiggle and shuffle by.
A shrimp tried to hop, but slipped on a stone,
Then laughed at himself; it's better alone!

A nimble snail raced, but he didn't get far,
With a cheer from a crab and a wink from a star.
"Life's quite a ride on this slippery ledge!"
Cried a plucky old sea urchin, stuck on the edge.

Echoes of the Ocean Floor

Down at the bottom, where treasures lay hid,
A clam shared a joke with a shy little squid.
"Why did the fish cross the coral at night?
To catch a bright dream, not to end up in fright!"

A starfish chimed in, "That's quite a good one!
I'd laugh too, but I'm stuck in the sun!"
So they all took a giggle, at the silliest lore,
Echoing laughter on the ocean floor.

Secrets of the Shimmering Tide

In the shallow water, crabs do dance,
With sideways shuffles, they take a chance.
A starfish pranks with its arms spread wide,
While little fish giggle, trying to hide.

Anemones wave in the splashy laugh,
While sea cucumbers take a deep bath.
A clam jokes loudly, 'I'm just a shell!'
But whispers of zany tales they tell.

The Pulse of the Ocean's Heart

Waves tumble in, with a giggle and spin,
A hermit crab's shell is the best place to win.
The jellyfish floats like a balloon on a spree,
While seagulls quack tales, sipping cups of sea.

A flounder grins, with both eyes on show,
'I'm flat-out hilarious,' it proudly will crow.
The seaweed sways with a snicker and wink,
As barnacles gather, they toast with a drink.

A Tapestry of Tides

Seashells gossip in a colorful queue,
While tiny shrimp play peekaboo.
A plucky octopus juggles with flair,
As gulls caw laughter into the air.

Starry nights bring glow to those moments,
When crabs share tales of funny opponents.
Lobsters complain of their crabby old fate,
'Why wear a shell when you can just skate?'

Discoveries at Water's Edge

At the water's edge, a treasure awaits,
With bubble-blowing fish and crabby debates.
A sea snail chuckles, moving quite slow,
'I'm on my own timeline, just thought you should know!'

The sea stars shine like bright, quirky pals,
While sand dollars float in extravagant gowns.
A surf clam shrieks, 'Don't take life too tight!'
And flips with a splash, it's a silly delight!

Layers of Life in the Lagoon

In the lagoon where critters play,
A crab does a dance, hip-hip-hooray!
With a swagger so grand, he waves his claw,
While fish roll their eyes, "What'd we just saw?"

A starfish tries hard to steal the show,
Doing cartwheels, oh what a flow!
The seaweed giggles, swaying so light,
While clams keep it quiet, hiding in fright.

A jellyfish floats by, full of grace,
Bumping into bubbles, oh what a race!
The sea cucumbers laugh with a sigh,
"Why swim when you can just float by?"

And crabs in a conga, a motley crew,
Sing a funny tune, just for you!
Underwater mischief, nothing too serious,
In layers of life, oh so delirious!

Whispers of the Aquatic Realm

In waters deep, where whispers cling,
A octopus wears a crown made of bling.
With tentacles waving, it reigns sublime,
While fish swim by, shouting, "That's not a crime!"

Anemones tickle the passing fish,
"Can you stop by for a quick squishy wish?"
But pufferfish puff up with a grin,
"Guys, not me! Just don't pull me in!"

A dolphin sings a silly melody,
While a lobster tells jokes, full of glee.
The sea turtles bicker on who's on track,
"Oh really, my back's not sore from that crack!"

With laughter echoing through coral halls,
Each creature adds to the murky brawls.
In the aquatic realm, fun takes the lead,
Every splash and giggle, a friendship's seed!

Enigmas in the Surf

In the shallows, crabs dance and prance,
They wave their claws, like they've found romance.
Sea urchins wear spikes like party hats,
While a starfish sings to the passing brats.

A jellyfish jiggles without a care,
Invisible, yet everywhere—oh, beware!
Seagulls squawk with their beak on a mission,
Who knew nature had such a goofy vision?

Clams hold their breath, wishing to be seen,
While shrimp play tag, feeling quite marine.
The ocean whispers secrets to the shore,
As treasures await just a bit offshore.

With waves that giggle and currents that tease,
Each splash a chuckle, a hum from the seas.
Come laugh with the critters beneath your toes,
In this salty world, where humor flows!

Flickers of Fitzgerald's Cove

In Fitzgerald's Cove, the fish wear ties,
They swim with swagger, what a surprise!
Octopuses juggle, their arms all a-twist,
While eels throw darts, oh, they can't be missed!

Seashells gossip about the crabs in stealth,
"Did you see Larry?" they cackle in wealth.
A seagull dives down for the fanciest fry,
Only to find it's just a passing guy!

Starfish have meetings, with no one in charge,
Debating the best way to be extra-large.
The surf sings a ditty, a catchy refrain,
As waves crack up laughter, again and again!

Lobsters wear shades, looking ever so cool,
They strut on the sand, making all the rules.
In this whimsical world where chuckles do gleam,
Life is a party, fishy and extreme!

Harmony of the Coastal Echo

In the whispers of foam, the clams are quite bold,
They tell tall tales of adventures untold.
A crab in a tux makes a dash for the dance,
While a fish in a top hat gives friendship a chance.

Anemones wave, with colors so bright,
Poking their heads in the morning light.
Starfish wear sandals, oh, such a delight,
Each wave that giggles wraps them up tight!

Seagulls are jesters, causing such fun,
They steal little snacks, oh, what have they done?
The tide plays a tune, a watery cheer,
As laughter pounds softly like a drum in your ear!

So spin with the tide, let your worries go,
In the coastal echo, you'll find quite the show.
For life near the surf is a treasure to keep,
Where funny delights make the sea creatures leap!

Life Where the Land Meets the Sea

Where the land greets the sea, it's a silly affair,
With otters that tumble as they frolic with flair.
Crabs race for cover, oh, what is that sound?
It's a wave of laughter from the sand all around!

The seals make a splash, not caring at all,
As they play leapfrog, with a splash and a call.
Seaweed wiggles, tickling those passing by,
While dolphins join in, leaping high to the sky!

Clownfish tell jokes, real comedians at heart,
While the stingrays glide with such elegant art.
Sand dollars giggle, tucked snug in their beds,
Amongst all these wonders, silly dreams spread.

So join in the fun, where sea and shore meet,
With each twist and turn, laughter flows like a sheet.
Life's a grand show on this vast, sandy spree,
Where joy rolls like waves, and all feel the glee!

Tide's Hidden Treasures

In a shell, a crab's a king,
Strutting sideways, what a fling!
Anemones dance, oh so spry,
While fishy jokes swim by and sigh.

A snail in slippers, oh what a sight,
Wearing a hat, quite snug and tight!
Barnacles whisper to clams nearby,
"Tide's our stage, come see us fly!"

A starfish flaunts a polka-dot spree,
Catching crabs on a hide-and-seek spree.
Each tide brings laughter, bubbling delight,
The ocean's a circus, day turns to night.

So when you stroll by the frothy foam,
Remember these giggles among the sea's dome.
With critters amusing and seaweed friends,
The fun never stops, the laughter transcends!

Portraits of Aquatic Life

A snail with shades lounges in sun,
While a fishy comedian jokes just for fun.
The octopus winks, all eight limbs ajar,
Judging a mullet with a snicker from afar.

Crabs hold a dance-off, claws raised high,
With barnacles cheering as they wave goodbye.
A starfish photobombs with glee,
"Can we all agree it's better at sea?"

Jellyfish bounce like balloons in a row,
Floating on whispers, they steal the show.
Mollusks with sass, shells shiny and bright,
Pose for portraits in shimmering light.

Flip through the pages, the tide tells their tale,
Of squawking seabirds loudly set sail.
Nutty encounters in each salty scene,
The ocean's alive with laughter unseen!

Lullabies of the Lapping Waves

The waves sing softly, a tickle and tease,
As crabs play tag with shadows and breeze.
A fish in pajamas floats down with grace,
While jellybeans spiral, a sweet little race.

Seagulls squawk silly lullabies loud,
Spreading their wings, they fall on the crowd.
Fish in pajamas with finned little feet,
Slide down the waves, a slippery treat.

Mollusks and seaweed sway to the tune,
While sea cucumbers dance under the moon.
Starfish giggle, their arms all aglow,
Dreaming of bubbles that twinkle below.

With sand-grain pillows tucked under the sky,
The sea's lullabies make all worries fly.
So close your eyes, let the ocean keep,
Its funny little secrets, a whimsical sleep!

Sea Stars in their Celestial Playground

Sea stars tumble, a cosmic delight,
Wrestling sea urchins, oh what a sight!
With twinkling eyes, they roll in the sand,
Turning the tide, they dream of a band.

Conch shells play music, a lovely refrain,
As the sea stars waltz, embracing the strain.
Anemone springs from behind a rock,
Saying, "Join the party, it's time to unlock!"

Caught in a swirl of laughter and light,
Barnacles clap, cheering with all their might.
Underwater shenanigans, silly and bright,
A kaleidoscope world, pure joy in sight.

Cosmic sea stars dance 'neath the waves,
While whispers of whimsy bring tales of the braves.
A delightful adventure where all are invited,
In the playground of ocean, joy is ignited!

Coastline Chronicles

In the sand, a crab's dance show,
He sidesteps left, oh what a pro!
With tiny claws and a sideways glance,
He shimmies and shakes, quite the prance!

A starfish snoozes, all spread out wide,
Dreams of the currents, a lazy tide.
But watch out, friend, a child nearby,
Is planting castles, oh my, oh my!

Seagulls squawk, they dive and swoop,
Snatchin' a snack, taking a loop.
As waves crash loud, laughter is heard,
Nature's circus, so absurd!

Who knew the beach was such a stage?
Full of antics, from age to age.
Join the fun, take off your shoes,
Embrace the joy, there's nothing to lose!

Treasures of the Underfoot

A mussel is grumpy, clinging so tight,
"Why'd you poke me? I'm not a delight!"
An octopus peeks with eight curious eyes,
"Can you see my skills? I'm full of surprises!"

Sand dollars flip in the sun with glee,
"Take us home, we're precious, you see!"
But a hermit crab laughs, in a borrowed shell,
"No one wants us, but we know it well!"

Tiny fish dart, in a dazzling race,
They giggle and bubble, oh, what a space!
A sea cucumber rolls, looking bemused,
"Why's everyone swimming? I'm just confused!"

So much life beneath every wave,
A wacky world, filled with the brave.
Step lightly, friend, there's fun to be found,
In the treasures hidden low to the ground!

The Poetry of Pebble and Wave

Pebbles argue on what is best,
"I'm the smoothest!" one puffs his chest.
"Not a chance, all agree, I'm the hero!"
As waves crash in for the big finale show!

A clam shouts back, "Hey, look at me,
I'm the master of clamming, can't you see?"
But a dolphin leaps, with a joyful spin,
"Who needs shells when I'm the kingpin?"

The seaweed sways, in an elegant dance,
Joining the laughter, giving a chance.
"Come, all ye critters, let's have some fun,
Under the rays of the sizzling sun!"

So gather your friends, let's make a scene,
With splashes and laughter, bright and serene.
Nature's poem, spoken in waves so clear,
With every tide, brings joy and cheer!

Awe Among the Anemones

An anemone waves, quite the flamboyant sight,
"Watch me, I'm dancing, isn't it right?"
But a clownfish scoffs, "You're just a plant,
Am I the star here? Give me a chant!"

An octopus grins, with a wink and a nod,
"I change my colors — go ahead, applaud!"
But the shrimp nearby, with a cheeky grin,
Sings, "You're just a chameleon, that's a sin!"

From sea cucumbers lost, in their own fun,
To crabs making faces — oh, everyone's spun!
"In this wild scene, who's the silliest of all?"
The laughter erupts like a jubilant call!

Each wave brings a tale, each shore has a jest,
Nature's comedians don't need a quest.
Join the antics, let down your hair,
Among the anemones, joy fills the air!

Beneath the Ocean's Veil

Little fish in disco shoes,
Dancing 'neath the waves, they cruise.
Crabs in tuxedos, snappy and spry,
Compliment the kelp in a wavy tie.

Starfish striking silly poses,
Debating what the ocean chose.
Seaweed sways, a chatty tree,
"Let's hold a party! Just you and me!"

Crustacean Chronicles

A lobster with a big, bold grin,
Said, "Who really needs a shell to win?"
He juggles clams, and crabs all cheer,
"Just another day on the coastline, dear!"

The shrimp parade with tiny hats,
Shouting out loud, "We're where it's at!"
But watch out for those fishy folks,
Their jokes are stale; they're really no yokes!

Reflections in a Rippled Pool

In a puddle where minnows play,
Frogs hop in and steal the show today.
"Can you swim? Come on, let's dive!"
The fish shout back, "We're barely alive!"

Snails on scooters, zooming by fast,
Making waves, while the seaweed laughs.
"Life's a race, who needs a trail?"
Just don't get stuck on the slimy snail!

The Color Palette of the Coast

Bright sea urchins in polka dot suits,
Claim they're now the style roots.
Octopus with a paintbrush, so bold,
Creating art in colors untold.

Anemones waltz about in delight,
Tickled by fish who dance through the night.
"This is our art," they all coo in glee,
A gallery here beneath the sea!

Shadows of the Seabed

Starfish playing hide and seek,
Bouncing on the sandy cheek.
Crabs don hats, oh what a sight,
Dance in the dark, then take flight.

Sea cucumbers in a race,
Slow and steady, set the pace.
Jellyfish float like clowns at play,
Wobbling through the salty spray.

Tiptoe close and hear them chat,
A clam says, 'Please, no more of that!'
Anemones wave, put on a show,
'Who tickled me? Come on, let's go!'

A starry night with critters bright,
Under waves, they giggle with delight.
The shadows laugh, they wave their fins,
In this deep sea world, the fun begins.

Sunlight on Shelled Secrets

Waves glimmer with a chuckling glee,
The sun plays tag with crab and sea.
Conch shells giggle, sharing tales,
Of snorkeling fish and wind-filled sails.

A hermit crab with a borrowed shell,
Said, 'I might just wear it well!'
Seagulls squawk about their bling,
Collecting treasures, oh what a fling!

Oysters laugh, pearls tucked away,
'Open up! Come play today!'
Starfish glare at the lazy sun,
'Wouldn't it be great to run?'

Under the light, secrets abound,
With every splash, a joy is found.
A beach party, where nothing's shy,
Dancing beneath the open sky.

Secrets in the Seaweed

In the green, the fish play tricks,
Wiggling tails with little licks.
Seaweed fans throw a party pass,
'Join us now, come shake your grass!'

A silly octopus shows his moves,
Twisting and turning, he's got the grooves.
Clinging crabs start a conga line,
Twist and shout, oh how they shine!

Kelp floats up to show it's sleek,
"We're the life of this fishy clique!"
Seahorses whinny while doing a jig,
Wiggling their tails, looking quite big!

Under the waves, they laugh and play,
In seaweed fields, they dance away.
With each silly swirl and giggly ploy,
The ocean's secrets create such joy.

Tales of the Castaway Coast

Upon the shore, a bottle floats,
A message sealed from fishy goats.
Pirate crabs with treasure maps,
Dream of gold in sandy traps.

Seagulls swoop with a cheeky squawk,
'Just a little further, let's take a walk!'
Oysters gossip, they're quite the fright,
'Oh my, did you see that dandy kite?'

A dolphin leaps, claims he's the king,
But the little fish roll, and say, 'Not a thing!'
Shells tell stories of glimmering tides,
Filled with laughter that never hides.

At sunset's end, the banners wave,
In this coastal kingdom, they're all quite brave.
Each tale shared and each laugh spilled,
Makes the castaway coast so fulfilled.

The Symphony of Shores

A hermit crab dances with flair,
In a shell that's too big, there's room to spare.
Anemones waltz, what a sight,
As sea stars twirl, they're out for a bite.

The seaweed's a wig, all tangled and grand,
As fish take the stage, a curious band.
A clam's sudden sneeze, oh what a surprise,
The whole crowd erupts with laughter and cries!

Seagulls squawk, they steal the scene,
While crabs throw shade, all laughing with glee.
In this ocean theater, chaos reigns,
Not a dull moment amidst all the gains!

As the sun sets down on this merry scene,
Even the barnacles look rather keen.
Each tide brings a tale, with actors so sly,
At the shore, it's a laugh, oh me, oh my!

A Day at the Water's Edge

A tiny fish swims, wearing bright shoes,
It bumps into snails, confused by the views.
The crabs are in fashion, wiggling with style,
While a starfish complains it's been stuck for a while.

A jellyfish floats, jelly wobbly and grand,
Hosting a party, it offers its hand.
The sea cucumbers, shy, wish to join in,
But alas, they're too busy, without much of a spin!

A pelican drops in, planning a dive,
Misjudging the wave—oh, to survive!
He flaps and he flops, it's a splashy affair,
While all of the clams try to maintain their flair!

Good news for all, the tide pulls back slow,
Bringing treasures unseen from below.
Together they giggle at the stories they share,
In the laughter of nature, there's joy everywhere!

Secrets of the Salty Shallows

In the salty shallows, laughter's the key,
A tug of war game with a driftwood debris.
The fish in their schools, wearing sparkly shrouds,
Pretend they're the kings, showing off to the clouds.

A curious octopus paints with its ink,
In hues of bright purple, what makes you think?
The sea urchins giggle, all spiky and bold,
While clowns in the kelp tell jokes to be told.

The hermit crabs chirp with a sidestep of flair,
In search of fresh shells, the latest fashion wear.
The flounder plays hide and seek with the rays,
While sand dollars wish to count down the days!

Echoes of laughter ride every wave,
As starfish join in, hoping to save.
The magic unravels with each little tease,
In the depths of the shallows, it's all just a breeze!

Beneath the Breaking Waves

Beneath breaking waves, a party unfolds,
With creatures galore, each story retold.
A crab with a crabby old face finds a shoe,
Wears it like royalty; that's just how crabs do!

A dolphin is diving with all of its might,
Encouraging seaweed to dance through the night.
With bubbles aplenty, they rise and they fall,
Making a splash that's out loud and tall!

Seahorses prance in a whimsical line,
While fish roll their eyes, making fun of their shine.
Anenomes giggle with ticklish delight,
As clownfish parade till the end of the night.

The tide whispers secrets to rocks on the floor,
Sharing old tales, oh, to laugh and explore!
In the laughter of life, the ocean's a sage,
With humor and mirth, it's a splendid stage!

The Lullaby of Oceanic Breezes

In a snug little nook, where the seaweed grows,
A crab wears a hat, striking quite the pose.
He dances a jig with a wink and a grin,
While fish roll their eyes, thinking he's quite thin.

A starfish sings softly with five tiny pipes,
While snails throw a party—oh, what silly types!
They laugh and they cheer, 'til the tide says, "Hey!"
And washes their fun all away, oh, hooray!

The Magic Beneath the Waves

A jellyfish floats, with flair and with style,
Wobbling around, like it's got a big smile.
The sea cucumbers giggle, oh what a sight,
As a clam tells a tale of a very brave fight.

Octopus dreams of a hat made of shells,
But instead finds an eel that gives quite the swells.
Together they squiggle, a silly parade,
Where bubbles burst laughter, and no one is afraid!

Timeless Tales of the Coast

A seagull in sandals struts on the sand,
Claiming the best shell—it's really quite grand.
A crab named Joe leaps, just trying to dance,
While a fish named Pierre throws him a chance.

They organize races, with seaweeds for stakes,
Beating the barnacles by all their mistakes.
As the tide comes up laughing, they all start to cheer,
For oceanic tales that bring joy near and dear!

Colorful Secrets of the Sea

A clownfish is giggling, it jokes with a shrimp,
Who's scared of a shadow that's shaped like a blimp.
They compare their colors, both bright as the sun,
While an enemy crab thinks he's quite the fun.

A sea horse in glasses reads quite the fine book,
'The Secrets of Sand' with an inquisitive look.
He chuckles and snorts with a bubble or two,
Sharing secrets with friends, as all good pals do!

The Saltwater Tapestry

In a beachside bowl, a crab spins about,
Trying to dance, but he flails with a shout.
A starfish complains, 'I've lost my best shoe!'
While a clownfish grins, 'Don't worry, I've two!'

The seaweed sways, a wiggly delight,
Whispers of shells, gossip late into night.
A turtle slips by, his shell painted bright,
Says, 'Type of swimwear? I call it just right!'

An octopus juggles with flair and with glee,
With jellyfish gas bags that float like a bee.
'Come join the fun!' the anemone calls,
As bubbles burst forth like wild carnival balls!

So here in this cauldron of color and cheer,
All creatures unite without worry or fear.
In nature's great show, both silly and grand,
Join in the dance with your toes in the sand!

Hidden Realms of the Riptide

Under a rock, in the muddy old muck,
Lives a crab with bad jokes, always in luck.
He tells of a fish who wore slippers too tight,
And danced with a sea lion all through the night!

A seahorse struts by, wearing shades and a grin,
While sea snails parade in their shell-traveling skin.
They sing silly songs of the beach and the foam,
'The ocean's our home, we'll never feel alone!'

The barnacles gossip, their stories the best,
Of a mermaid who couldn't find her sea guest.
They say she was looking for love in the tide,
But tripped on a clam and barely survived!

So gather your laughter, your seashells, your pride,
There's magic and mayhem beneath every stride.
With friends who make waves, and giggles galore,
These hidden realms open wide every shore!

Wonders in the Wavy World

Oysters in pearls, who think they're the best,
Scoff at the clams, from their gritty little nest.
'You shine like a dime,' one clam shouted back,
'But I'm tougher than leather, so watch your attack!'

A playful seal flips, performing with flair,
While krill keep the beat in a fabulous square.
A dolphin comes leaping, all laughter and light,
'Who needs dolphins on TV? We're quite the sight!'

With plankton confetti that dances in air,
The party rolls on, it's quite the affair!
The fish all unite, forming conga lines,
Each twist and each turn a tale to divine!

So raise up your fins and wiggle your toes,
In this wavy world where the laughter just grows.
With creatures like these, who need a long shore?
We're all sporting our fins, never a bore!

Life Between the Waves

In a world made of bubbles, clams play with pride,
While squids set the mood with their ink and their glide.
A fish on a surfboard, oh what a sight,
Goes zooming by fast in a splash of pure light!

The turtles race by, in their shells really neat,
But crabs are convinced they'll admit defeat.
'We're speedy,' they squeak, with pincers held high,
'In this dance of the tides, we'll surely comply!'

A pufferfish's tale brings laughter and fun,
'When I blow up big, I'm the life of the pun!'
While urchins all chuckle in prickly delight,
'This underwater circus is just outta sight!'

So swim through this splash with a grin on your face,
In the whirl of the waves, there's plenty of space.
With giggles and wiggles, the sea's full of glee,
Together we bounce in the ocean's jubilee!

Creations in Coastal Currents

A crab in a hat dances with glee,
Waving his claws, quite fancy, you see.
A starfish who thinks he can sing like a star,
Screeches out notes that go way off far.

The fish wear a tie for their weekly debate,
Discussing the best ways to dance with their fate.
But a seagull swoops in, trying to be sly,
Snatching their lunch while they ponder why.

An octopus juggles with pearls and with flair,
While snails play the drums with shells from their lair.
Laughter erupts from a startled sea urchin,
Who quips, "Next time, bring snacks for certain!"

With laughter and joy, the waves start to sway,
As the tide brings new friends to join in their play.
They all wave goodbye, till the next ocean spin,
Hoping for tides that bring more fun within.

A Dream of Drift

A plankton parade floats under the moon,
Dressed in tiny robes, they sway to the tune.
Seaweed swirls, like a dancer on stage,
Spinning around with a marvelous rage.

A fish with a mustache prances in cheer,
Chasing a bubble that floats ever near.
"Catch me if you can!" he giggles with glee,
But the bubble just pops, oh silly fishy!

The sandy bottom hosts a slippery race,
Where hermit crabs battle to find the best place.
Each swapping their shells like they're hats at a fair,
With thrilling remarks that float through the air.

As the tide sweeps away their sandy abode,
They laugh and they dance on their unpaved road.
For in soft, salty dreams, they know it's not done,
Tomorrow's another day filled with fun!

A Dance of Tide

A dolphin leaps high, dressed up in a bow,
Pretending it's fancy as if in a show.
The fish do the cha-cha, all shiny and bright,
While seahorses twist, with a delicate light.

Crabs in a conga, they shuffle and slide,
Clicking their claws, they take it in stride.
Anemones blush at their wild, silly sight,
And jellyfish giggle, drifting left and right.

A picnic is set, with seaweed the spread,
With barnacle butter, and jellyfish bread.
The oysters all cheer as they twist and they turn,
Each pearl gets a dance, it's their time to burn!

With laughter and joy, the currents invite,
A dance through the deep, till the end of the night.
For beneath the blue waves, life's nothing but cheer,
Each moment a dance, with nothing to fear.

Cradled by the Sea's Embrace

A whale has a teacup, it's quite a sight,
Sipping on krill while trying to take flight.
A penguin in shades slides down a wet rock,
Claiming his treasure, a bright, shiny sock.

Clams have a meeting, deciding the fate,
Of who has the shell that's simply first-rate.
While gulls critique their most recent parade,
Saying, "Ah, that's not the shell that we've made!"

The current provides a delightful buffet,
With snacks that are dancing and singing hooray.
A flotilla of fish forms a swirling array,
While a starfish plays cool on a sunny day.

With splashes of joy and bubbles of fun,
The sea laughs and plays, till the day is all done.
For in this grand ocean, we've all found our place,
With silly little moments in a watery space.

Fragility in Fluid Colors

An urchin in pink paints the coral anew,
While anemones giggle, saying, "Look at you!"
A pufferfish ponders a balloon's nice allure,
Till he pops it right off, "Oops! How demure!"

Butterfly fish flutter, in suits full of zest,
Debating who shines the most in this fest.
An octopus watches, with shades on its head,
Whispering softly, "Now who's gotten fed?"

Sea cucumbers lounge on a float made of foam,
"Let's make it a party, we're far from our home!"
As turtles do backflips, the laughter erupts,
While jellyfish whirl, and the joy just erupts.

Oh, the days are exciting when living so free,
In colors and textures, a whimsical spree.
Each creature unique, on this vibrant stage,
Dancing and laughing, life's all the rage!

Coral Gardens at Dusk

In coral homes, the fish do sway,
A wriggling dance at close of day.
A crab in a suit, all snazzy and spry,
Claims he's the king under the pink sky.

Anemones wave, quite proud of their flair,
While snails take their time, without a care.
Starfish gossip while barnacles snooze,
Whispering secrets in fuchsia hues.

The octopus tries to juggle and flail,
But drops his catch, it's quite the fail!
Bubbles of laughter rise from the deep,
As seaweed sways, the jokes run steep.

In this coral dream, where humor swells,
Even the clams have funny tales to tell.
With laughter and colors, the dusk's delight,
A comical end to a vibrant night.

The Artistry of Aquatic Shadows

Deep in the waves, shadows play tag,
With squishy surprises in every bag.
A jellyfish floats, a real acrobat,
Doing swim tricks in a floppy hat.

Hermit crabs bicker, they're quite the bunch,
Arguing over who's got the best lunch.
One boasts of pearls, the other of snails,
While clams roll their eyes at their silly tales.

The sea cucumber does a slow-motion slide,
While fish race by in a colorful ride.
Bubble-blowing turtles have quite the show,
With giggles and wiggles as they steal the flow.

As shadows dance under the moon's embrace,
Even the seaweed has a comical grace.
Artistry flows where the shadows convene,
In this wacky world, where giggles are seen.

Gems of the Intertidal Zone

Look at the rocks, a shiny delight,
With critters galore that dart out of sight.
A hermit crab's home, a treasure to find,
While sea stars lounge, utterly maligned.

Oysters wear pearls, they strut with pride,
While wiggly worms take a swell, silly ride.
Sea urchins poke, with grins on their face,
Inviting all critters to join in the race.

Clownfish bob like they're out for a stroll,
Finding new friends to keep them whole.
Little crabs pinch in a friendly mock,
Creating a scene that totally rocks!

Among all the gems of the ocean's small space,
Laughter and joy put a smile on each face.
In this quirky realm, hilarity blooms,
As creatures of whimsy lift our glooms.

Tide's Embrace

When the waves rush in, it's a playful embrace,
Sea creatures tumble, all over the place.
A dolphin surfaces, flipping with glee,
While flounders just lie, with no need to flee.

Seashells gather, gossiping loud,
"Did you see that tide? It's becoming a crowd!"
Gulls cackle above, on a mission to tease,
As sea cucumbers sway in the breeze.

Starfish attempt a moonlit ballet,
Falling in heaps in a hilarious way.
The kelp sways like it's lost in a trance,
Inviting all critters to join in the dance.

With every splash, laughter rings clear,
In the arms of the tide, there's nothing to fear.
So let's splash away, till the daylight's done,
In this watery world, where we all have fun!

Echoes of the Incoming Wave

The seaweed shakes, a dance so grand,
Crabs wear hats made from the sand.
A fishy joke is shared with glee,
As twinkling shells shout, "Look at me!"

The barnacles cheer with tiny rhymes,
While snails take naps, counting their times.
Anemones giggle, waving their arms,
To every tide's push, they share their charms.

A starfish slips, he can't find his shoe,
And whispers, "Hey, I lost my clue!"
The sea cucumber laughs, rolling along,
In this crazy dance, we all belong.

With bubbles tickling, the sea floor smiles,
Creatures unite in their goofy styles.
Echoes of laughter float on the breeze,
At this beach party, it's all just a tease.

Starfish Dreams Beneath the Surface

A starfish yawns in a dreamy chill,
Imagining adventures, oh what a thrill!
With five little arms, he stretches out wide,
Dreams of funny fish dancing with pride.

Meanwhile, octopus scribbles a note,
"I need a new hat, or maybe a coat!"
With every swish, he colors the sea,
Creating a fashion so wild and free.

"A crab stole my sunglasses," he muses in jest,
"I'll challenge him now, give it my best!"
But alas, he's tangled in all of his ink,
Creating a masterpiece, quicker than you think.

In this underwater world of schemes,
Every creature is lost in their dreams.
Starfishes giggle, deep down in the blue,
We're all just wishing for something new!

Journey Through Rocky Realms

Through rocky realms where the critters play,
Every pebble hides a secret ballet.
Puffing pufferfish don't want to be shy,
They blow up like balloons, oh my, oh my!

Lobsters strut with their claws held high,
Telling tall tales of the fish that swim by.
Sea urchins chuckle, prickly and round,
In this rocky wonderland, joy can be found.

A hermit crab's lost his cozy abode,
Now wearing a soda can, on the road.
He laughs and shuffles, what a sight, what a show!
In this journey, there's always a glow.

But beware of the octopus trying to tease,
With a wig made of seaweed, just to please.
Every twist and turn in this rocky space,
Holds giggles of creatures, a wild embrace.

Dances of the Sea Slug

Oh the sea slug slides in a wobbly way,
With colors so bright, it brightens the day.
He shakes and he wobbles, a wiggly dance,
As nearby fish stop and take a glance.

He twirls with a jelly and spins with a crab,
Making up moves that are totally fab.
The other sea critters can't help but grin,
At the fabulous fun that he's dancing in.

A seahorse joins in, with a flip and a sway,
Together they boogie, what a joyful display!
The kelp starts to sway, keeping the beat,
As everyone's feet (or fins) feel the heat.

With laughter and bubbles, they all come alive,
In a raucous routine, watch them thrive!
These dances of sea slugs, so funny and sweet,
Make even the seals want to get on their feet.

Celestial Creatures of the Coast

The starfish twirls in a lazy dance,
A crab with a hat takes a bold chance.
With one little claw, he waves and he winks,
While a sea cucumber quietly thinks.

The octopus dons a snazzy bow tie,
Pretending to sing while the seagulls fly by.
A prancing sea slug, what an odd sight,
In this coastal circus, all feels just right.

The sand dollars giggle, buried in sand,
As jellyfish glide, with grace they expand.
Anemones wave in a rainbow display,
In this underwater cabaret, they play.

So come take a peek, with your eyes really wide,
At the comical creatures that flourish in tide!
For in this wet wonder, where laughter's the key,
There's joy in the ocean, just wait and you'll see.

The Lure of Barnacle Clusters

Barnacles cling like gossiping friends,
Holding tight together with no plans to end.
They share all the tales that the waves let them hear,
Each crusty little wedge full of gossip and cheer.

With a barnacle hat, a clam makes a splash,
As crabs join the rumor, they all start to clash.
The barnacles chuckle, as waves come and go,
While a lazy old clam, just enjoys the show.

Barnacle balls jest, in a sticky embrace,
Holding on dearly, to their sandy place.
While the tide keeps on rolling, their antics take flight,
In a sticky situation, they laugh through the night.

So next time you wander, and spot a weak shell,
Remember the gossip that barnacles tell.
For laughter's in clusters, while we splash in the foam,
In the crazy briny waters, we all find our home.

Wave-Kissed Wonders

A fish in sunglasses swims by with a grin,
While a turtle in flip-flops starts kicking it in.
The waves crash and roll, what a raucous delight,
As seagulls belting tunes take to the sky bright.

A group of shrimp play a game of charades,
Imitating fishermen, all in cascades.
A starfish says, "Hey, watch my wild moves!"
As barnacles cheer from their stony grooves.

The seaweed blows kisses, swaying with glee,
As crabs join a conga, both funny and free.
Wave-kissed and silly, their antics abound,
In this salty wonder, where joy can be found.

So hop on a wave, let your laughter ignite,
In a parade of the ocean, let's dance through the night.
For under the surface, where wonder can dwell,
Let the tide of hilarity rise and compel.

Portraits of a Marine Mosaic

In waters of blue, the snails take their place,
With smiles made of shells, they join in the race.
The clams call for harmony, all in good jest,
While a quirky old lobster attempts his best.

An urchin with spikes, stands out from the crowd,
With a wink and a grin, he is feeling so proud.
Mollusks gather round for the underwater show,
As fish flip and flop, with a hint of a glow.

A mural of colors beneath the bright sun,
Is a concert of laughter, where all are having fun.
The sea cucumbers twirl, their moves quite a sight,
While a piggyback shrimp hitches a ride, oh what a flight!

So if you're ever near, take a moment to see,
This mosaic of life, where there's joy to be.
For humor's alive in the ocean so wide,
In a canvas of laughter, let happiness glide.

Secrets in the Briny Depths

In the splash of the waves, there's a tale untold,
A crab with a hat, oh so bold!
He sips from a shell, like a sassy king,
While the fish roll their eyes at this ridiculous fling.

A starfish recites poetry, oh what a hoot,
While sea cucumbers dance in their suit.
The jellyfish giggle with glee and delight,
As the seaweed sways in the soft, calming light.

An octopus juggles, his arms spread out wide,
Throwing clams in the air—what a comical ride!
With each shocking splash, the turtles can't breathe,
As they roll in the sand, "Let's just take our leave!"

In this rocky retreat, where laughter won't cease,
Secrets of joy are found in the breeze.
So come join the fun in the bath of the sea,
Where every kind creature is silly and free!

Marvelous Minions of the Coast

Under the yellow sun, in the salty domain,
Little critters are ready to entertain.
With goggles and fins, they splash with a cheer,
The minions of mischief are all gathered here.

A clam throws a fit, waving his shell with pride,
While seagulls are cackling, "Just look at that guy!"
The barnacles form a rock band so bold,
Playing groovy tunes that are funny yet old.

A shrimp with a trumpet has taken the stage,
While sea urchins crowd with a laugh and engage.
The sandy ginormous sea stars clap along,
To the rhythm of bubbles, they hum a new song.

But wait! What is that? A wave comes to crash,
Leaving all of our stars in a comical clash.
In this carnival sea, the fun's never glum,
For life here is silly, and joy's just begun!

Journey Through Saltwater Sanctuaries

In shallow pools where critters peek,
A crab with attitude starts to speak.
"I'm the king of this sandy throne,
With a sideways walk, I claim my zone!"

Starfish lounge on rocks with style,
Waving arms that stretch a mile.
"A high five? No, a six-legged twist!
Come join the party, you won't want to miss!"

School of fish takes a loop-de-loop,
Trying to impress a curious soup.
With a splash and a dart, they play tag,
Watch out, or you might get a fishy wag!

A sea urchin rolls and joins the fun,
"I'm not a ball; I'm just on the run!"
Quirky moments under the sun,
In this salty world, there's never a shun!

Secrets of the Shimmering Shells

Shells like treasures hide on the sand,
Whispers of stories, hand in hand.
A winkle-snail whispers with flair,
"I'm wearing my home; it's quite the affair!"

A hermit crab dips in and out,
"Is this my house? I'm filled with doubt!"
He switches shells like fancy hats,
"This one's perfect; it suits my spats!"

Clams with dreams of being a star,
"I'll take a bow before you, from afar!"
They giggle and shimmer as waves entice,
The ocean's a stage, and they're all quite nice!

Mollusks applaud, their shells all aglow,
"What a show! Bravo! Let's steal the show!"
In this secret haven, each finds a role,
A shell-abration, it fills the soul!

Harbor for the Hidden

Among the rocks, a secret galore,
Creatures hiding, always wanting more.
"I'm not just a rock, I'm a home sweet home!"
Said the shrimp, who'd prefer to roam.

Octopus giggling, changing hue,
"Am I here? Or am I still blue?"
With a wiggly dance and a playful spin,
Tugging at cephalopod kin!

Barnacles argue over prime real estate,
"I saw it first! You'll just have to wait!"
They cling and cling, with a chalky grin,
In their little fortress, they thrive with a spin!

Crabby neighbors start to complain,
"Why all the ruckus? You're driving me insane!"
But in the harbor, camaraderie reigns,
Hidden in laughter, that's where joy remains!

Refuge of the Resilient

In a nook where the tide sways low,
Creatures gather for a funny show.
"Don't mind my coat; it's just a little dry,
Blame my trip out—oh, the sky was shy!"

Worms wiggle in with tales to share,
"We're the artists; we dig with flair!"
They trail behind like ribbons in sand,
Wiggling and giggling, all hand in hand.

Anemones wave like they're at a dance,
"Join our ball; we'll give it a chance!"
Starfish stand guard with their five-point cheer,
"The best seat in the house is right over here!"

Tide's coming in, but they don't despair,
"We'll ride the waves; we're light as air!"
In every puddle, there's joy to reveal,
In a refuge of laughter, life is surreal!

Dreamscapes of Coral and Shell

In the splashy depths, a crab took a bow,
He wore a fancy shell, all shiny and wow.
A sea star danced with a snail on the run,
The ocean's a circus, and it's all just for fun.

Anemones giggled, as fish zoomed in haste,
"Who needs a ticket? There's plenty of space!"
A seahorse waltzed, with a flick of its tail,
"Catch me if you can!" it shouted with zeal.

Guilty are the clams, who hide in the sand,
In their secret world, they've got quite the band.
The hermit crabs gossip, all tucked in their homes,
"Who knew the world outside was so full of gnomes?"

So under the waves, where the silly ones play,
Life's full of laughter, come join in the fray!
For every odd creature with a grin on its face,
Makes diving for treasures a comical race.

Wonders of the Salted Shore

Upon the shore where the laughter's in waves,
A gull stole a sandwich, the joke's on the braves.
With a flap and a squawk, it took off like a jet,
In this game of the shore, it's hard to forget!

A jellyfish jiggled as it bobbed on the tide,
"Don't touch me, my friends!" it earnestly cried.
A crab cracked a joke, "Come and have a snack,
Just watch for my pinch, or I'll come for your back!"

The starfish stood firm, with a grin hard to see,
"Life's great when you're lazy, just look at me!"
A dolphin rolled in, saying "Catch me if you can!"
But tripped on a wave—what a wobbly plan!

The shore is a party, with laughter afloat,
As seaweed waves hello in a floaty boat.
Grab a bucket, some sand, make a castle with flair,
We'll rule the salty kingdom without a single care!

Where the Land and Sea Embrace

At the edge of the sand, where the two sides kiss,
A crab made a wish for a life full of bliss.
A clam rolled its eyes, "What a silly old chap,
Do crabs ever really know how to nap?"

A dolphin popped up, with a splash and a cheer,
Said, "Join us down here, the fun's crystal clear!"
"Jump into the surf! There's so much we can do,
I'll show you a trick—like flying, woo-hoo!"

The octopus knitted, with its many fine arms,
Scarves that water spirits would wear for their charms.
The shore critters laughed, "Fashion's not for the fish!"
While a seagull eyed lunch, with a rather sly swish.

So here on the fringe, where land meets the sea,
Laughter's the language, our spirits run free.
Embrace the odd moments, the silliness too,
Because life's a grand game, let's play it with you!

Echoes of Life Among the Tide

The tide rolled in laughter, as minnows took flight,
With a flip and a wiggle, such a comical sight.
A clam grumbled low, "Shhh, I'm trying to think!"
While a sea otter giggled, sipping on a drink.

An anemone waved, "Come play in my curls!"
While shrimps hit the dance floor, twirling in swirls.
A sand dollar sighed, "Oh why can't I dance?"
In a world full of joy, it still longs for a chance!

"Watch me!" cried a crab, doing backflips galore,
While a turtle just chuckled, and waved from the shore.
A fish with big dreams, swam up with a wink,
"How do you settle an argument? Just take a drink!"

Echoes of laughter roll over the shallows,
Chasing away worries, like philanthropic gallows.
In this life undersea, quirky charms reign supreme,
Dive in and enjoy, ride the laughter-filled stream!

www.ingramcontent.com/pod-product-compliance
Lightning Source LLC
Chambersburg PA
CBHW060142230426
43661CB00003B/540